SEASHORE SANCTUARIES

New York

1. Block Island National Wildlife Refuge (NWR)
2. Bluff Point State Park & Coastal Reserve
3. Great Meadows Marsh Area
4. Long Island NWR Complex
5. Jamaica Bay Wildlife Refuge
6. Wallkill River NWR
7. Edwin B. Forsythe NWR
8. Cape May NWR
9. Assateague Island National Seashore
10. Presquile NWR
11. Back Bay NWR
12. Pea Island NWR
13. Cape Hatteras & Cape Lookout National Seashores
14. Cedar Island NWR
15. Fort Fisher State Recreation Area
16. Huntington Beach State Park
17. Cape Romain NWR
18. Savannah NWR
19. Wassaw NWR
20. Gray's Reef National Marine Sanctuary
21. Cumberland Island National Seashore

Waterford Press produces reference guides that introduce novices to nature, science, survival and outdoor recreation. Product information is featured on the website:
www.waterfordpress.com

Text and illustrations © 2020 by Waterford Press Inc. All rights reserved.
Cover images © iStock Photo, Shutterstock. To order, call 800-434-2555.
For permissions, or to share comments, e-mail editor@waterfordpress.com.
For information on custom-published products, call 800-434-2555 or e-mail info@waterfordpress.com.

Made in the USA

ISBN 978-1-62005-468-0 $7.95 U.S.

EASTERN SEASHORE LIFE

A Waterproof Folding Guide to Familiar Animals & Plants

SEASHORE PLANTS

Glasswort
Salicornia spp.
To 18 in. (45 cm)
Greenish stems turn red-orange in autumn.

Sea Oats
Uniola paniculata
To 5 ft. (1.5 m)

Eelgrass
Zostera marina
To 4 ft. (1.2 m)

Sea Lettuce
Ulva lactuca To 26 in. (65 cm)

Sugar Kelp
Laminaria saccharina
To 15 ft. (4.5 m)

Sargassum
Sargassum spp.
To 33 ft. (10 m)

Chenille Weed
Dasya pedicellata
To 2 ft. (60 cm)
Found below low tide line in quiet waters.

Southern Bayberry
Myrica cerifera
To 30 ft. (9 m)
Common on wet and well-drained soils.
Fruits have a waxy coating and were once used to make candles.

Seaside Goldenrod
Solidago sempervirens
To 8 ft. (2.4 m)
Grows in sandy soil and salt marshes.

Beach Rose
Rosa rugosa
To 6 ft. (1.8 m)
Grows along shorelines.

Beach Plum
Prunus maritima
To 6 ft. (1.8 m)

Yaupon
Ilex vomitoria
To 20 ft. (6 m)

Sea Lavender
Limonium carolinianum
To 2 ft. (60 cm)

Prickly Pear Cactus
Opuntia spp.
Pads to 12 in. (30 cm)

MOLLUSKS

Hooked Mussel
Ischadium recurvum
To 2 in. (5 cm)

Lettered Olive
Oliva sayana
To 2.5 in. (6 cm)
Marks on shell resemble lettering.

Atlantic Ribbed Mussel
Geukensia demissa
To 5 in. (13 cm)

Blue Mussel
Mytilus edulis
To 4 in. (10 cm)
Grows attached to pilings and other marine objects.

Atlantic Auger
Terebra dislocata
To 2 in. (5 cm)

Soft-shelled Clam
Mya arenaria
To 6 in. (15 cm)

Shark Eye
Polinices duplicatus
To 2.5 in. (6 cm)

Common Slipper Snail
Crepidula fornicata
To 2 in. (5 cm)

Wentletrap
Epitonium spp.
To 2 in. (5 cm)
Shell has raised ridges.

Atlantic Bay Scallop
Argopecten irradians
To 3 in. (8 cm)

Eastern Oyster
Crassostrea virginica
To 10 in. (25 cm)

Angel Wing
Cyrtopleura costata
To 8 in. (20 cm)

Northern Moon Snail
Lunatia heros
To 4.5 in. (11 cm)

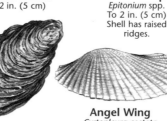

Giant Atlantic Cockle
Dinocardium robustum
To 5 in. (13 cm)

Channeled Whelk
Busycon canaliculatum
To 7 in. (18 cm)

Common Eastern Jingle Shell
Anomia simplex
To 2.5 in. (6 cm)

MOLLUSKS

Saw-toothed Pen Shell
Atrina serrata
To 10 in. (25 cm)

Atlantic Oyster Drill
Urosalpinx cinerea
To 1.25 in. (3.6 cm)
Feeds primarily on oysters.

Scotch Bonnet
Phalium granulatum
To 4 in. (10 cm)

Amethyst Gem Clam
Gemma gemma
To .3 in. (.8 cm)

Atlantic Surf Clam
Spisula solidissima
To 7 in. (18 cm)

Common Purple Sea Snail
Janthina janthina
To .75 in. (2 cm)

Northern Quahog
Mercenaria mercenaria
To 5 in. (13 cm)
Found in mud near low tide mark.

Sunray Venus Clam
Macrocallista nimbosa
To 5 in. (13 cm)

Common Baby's Ear
Sinum perspectivum
To 2 in. (5 cm)

Mottled Dog Whelk
Nassarius vibex
To .5 in. (1.3 cm)

Eastern Mud Whelk
Ilynassa obsoletus
To 1 in. (3 cm)

Coquina Clam
Donax variabilis
To .75 in. (2 cm)
Color is variable.

Common Razor Clam
Ensis directus
To 10 in. (25 cm)

Alternate Tellin
Tellina alternata
To 3 in. (8 cm)

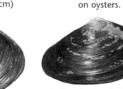

BEACH DRIFT

Sea Urchin Skeleton

Sand Dollar Skeleton

Skate Egg Case

SEA STARS, URCHINS & ALLIES

Atlantic Purple Sea Urchin
Arbacia punctulata
Body to 2 in. (5 cm)

Moon Jellyfish
Aurelia aurita
To 16 in. (40 cm)

Common Sea Star
Asterias forbesi
To 10 in. (25 cm)
May be tan, brown, orange or olive with orange highlights.

Sea Nettle
Chrysaora quinquecirrha
To 10 in. (25 cm)

Frilled Anemone
Metridium senile
To 18 in. (45 cm)

Keyhole Urchin
Mellita quinquiesperforata
To 6 in. (15 cm)

CRUSTACEANS

Horseshoe Crab
Limulus polyphemus
To 12 in. (30 cm) wide

Blue Crab
Callinectes sapidus
To 9 in. (23 cm)

Spider Crab
Libinia spp.
To 4 in. (10 cm)

Mole Crab
Emerita spp.
To 1 in. (3 cm)

Ghost Crab
Ocypode quadrata
To 2 in. (5 cm)

Fiddler Crab
Uca spp.
To 1.5 in. (4 cm)

Atlantic Rock Crab
Cancer irroratus
To 1.3 in. (3.6 cm)

Hermit Crab
Pagurus spp. To 1.3 in. (3.6 cm)
Lives in discarded shells.

NEARSHORE FISHES

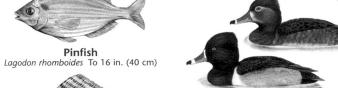

Spiny Dogfish
Squalus acanthias To 5 ft. (1.5 m)

Sea Lamprey
Petromyzon marinus To 33 in. (83 cm)
Found in fresh and salt water.

Northern Pipefish
Syngnathus fuscus To 12 in. (30 cm)

Striped Anchovy
Anchoa hepsetus To 6 in. (15 cm)

American Shad
Alosa sapidissima To 30 in. (75 cm)
Note line of spots behind gill cover.

American Eel
Anguilla rostrata To 5 ft. (1.5 m)
Snake-like fish has long dorsal and anal fins.

Atlantic Menhaden
Brevoortia tyrannus To 18 in. (45 cm)

Striped Bass
Morone saxatilis To 6 ft. (1.8 m)
Has 6-9 dark side stripes.

Pinfish
Lagodon rhomboides To 16 in. (40 cm)

Atlantic Herring
Clupea harengus To 18 in. (45 cm)

Sailfin Molly
Poecilia latipinna To 5 in. (13 cm)
Male has large, orange-edged dorsal fin.

Northern Puffer
Sphoeroides maculatus To 10 in. (25 cm)
Inflates body as a means of defense.

Flounder
Paralichthys spp. To 4 ft. (1.2 m)
Several similar species are found in shallow water.

Spotted Seatrout
Cynoscion nebulosus To 28 in. (70 cm)
Note spots on back, second dorsal fin and tail.

Black Drum
Pogonias cromis To 6 ft. (1.8 m)
Has prominent chin barbels.

Clearnose Skate
Raja eglanteria To 3 ft. (90 cm)

BIRDS

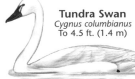

Tundra Swan
Cygnus columbianus To 4.5 ft. (1.4 m)

Pied-billed Grebe
Podilymbus podiceps To 13 in. (33 cm)
Note banded white bill.

Horned Grebe
Podiceps auritus To 15 in. (38 cm)

Canada Goose
Branta canadensis To 45 in. (1.14 m)

American Wigeon
Mareca americana 23 in. (58 cm)

Northern Pintail
Anas acuta To 30 in. (75 cm)

Ring-necked Duck
Aythya collaris 18 in. (45 cm)
Note white ring near bill tip.

Wood Duck
Aix sponsa To 20 in. (50 cm)

Mallard
Anas platyrhynchos To 28 in. (70 cm)

Northern Shoveler
Spatula clypeata To 20 in. (50 cm)
Named for its large spatulate bill.

Blue-winged Teal
Spatula discors To 16 in. (40 cm)

Green-winged Teal
Anas crecca To 15 in. (38 cm)

BIRDS

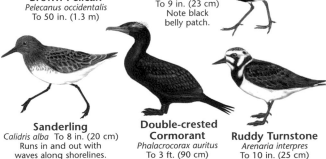

Common Goldeneye
Bucephala clangula To 18 in. (45 cm)
Male has a white facial spot.

Common Merganser
Mergus merganser To 27 in. (68 cm)
Note thin bill.

Bufflehead
Bucephala albeola To 15 in. (38 cm)

Lesser Scaup
Aythya affinis To 18 in. (45 cm)
Note peaked crown.

Canvasback
Aythya valisineria To 2 ft. (60 cm)
Note sloping forehead and black bill.

American Black Duck
Anas rubripes To 25 in. (63 cm)

Ruddy Duck
Oxyura jamaicensis To 16 in. (40 cm)
Often cocks tail when swimming.

White-winged Scoter
Melanitta fusca To 23 in. (58 cm)
Note white wing patches.

Brown Pelican
Pelecanus occidentalis To 50 in. (1.3 m)

Dunlin
Calidris alpina To 9 in. (23 cm)
Note black belly patch.

Sanderling
Calidris alba To 8 in. (20 cm)
Runs in and out with waves along shorelines.

Double-crested Cormorant
Phalacrocorax auritus To 3 ft. (90 cm)

Ruddy Turnstone
Arenaria interpres To 10 in. (25 cm)

BIRDS

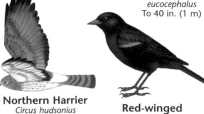

Spotted Sandpiper
Actitis macularius To 8 in. (20 cm)
Breast is spotted.

Killdeer
Charadrius vociferus To 12 in. (30 cm)
Note two breast bands.

Lesser Yellowlegs
Tringa flavipes To 10 in. (25 cm)

Green Heron
Butorides virescens To 22 in. (55 cm)

Willet
Tringa semipalmata To 17 in. (43 cm)

Semipalmated Plover
Charadrius semipalmatus To 8 in. (20 cm)
Note single breast band.

Great Blue Heron
Ardea herodias To 4.5 ft. (1.4 m)

American Coot
Fulica americana To 16 in. (40 cm)

Common Gallinule
Gallinula galeata To 14 in. (35 cm)

Belted Kingfisher
Megaceryle alcyon To 14 in. (35 cm)

White Ibis
Eudocimus albus To 28 in. (70 cm)
Juveniles are brownish.

Marsh Wren
Cistothorus palustris To 5 in. (13 cm)

American Oystercatcher
Haematopus palliatus To 20 in. (50 cm)

Black-crowned Night-Heron
Nycticorax nycticorax To 28 in. (70 cm)

Long-billed Curlew
Numenius americanus To 26 in. (65 cm)
Long bill is slightly downturned.

BIRDS

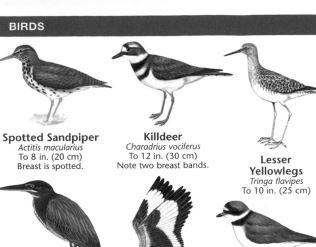

Forster's Tern
Sterna forsteri
Note forked tail and white wing tips.

Great Egret
Ardea alba To 38 in. (95 cm)
Note yellow bill and black feet.

Snowy Egret
Egretta thula To 26 in. (65 cm)
Note black bill and yellow feet.

Great Black-backed Gull
Larus marinus To 32 in. (80 cm)
Told by large size and dark back.

Common Tern
Sterna hirundo To 15 in. (38 cm)
Note black cap and forked tail. Orange bill is black-tipped.

Laughing Gull
Leucophaeus atricilla To 18 in. (45 cm)

Royal Tern
Thalasseus maximus To 22 in. (55 cm)
Orange bill and black head crest are key field marks.

Herring Gull
Larus argentatus To 26 in. (65 cm)
Legs are pinkish.

Ring-billed Gull
Larus delawarensis To 20 in. (50 cm)
Bill has dark ring.

Osprey
Pandion haliaetus To 2 ft. (60 cm)

Seaside Sparrow
Ammodramus maritimus To 6 in. (15 cm)

Bald Eagle
Haliaeetus eucocephalus To 40 in. (1 m)

Fish Crow
Corvus ossifragus To 20 in. (50 cm)

Northern Harrier
Circus hudsonius To 22 in. (55 cm)
Note V-shaped flight profile and white rump.

Red-winged Blackbird
Agelaius phoeniceus To 9 in. (23 cm)

REPTILES & AMPHIBIANS

Black Rat Snake
Elaphe obsoleta obsoleta To 8 ft. (2.4 m)

Northern Water Snake
Nerodia sipedon To 4.5 ft. (1.4 m)

Eastern Garter Snake
Thamnophis sirtalis sirtalis To 4 ft. (1.2 m)

Diamondback Terrapin
Malaclemys terrapin To 9 in. (23 cm)

Green Frog
Lithobates clamitans To 4 in. (10 cm)

Eastern Fence Lizard
Sceloporus undulatus To 8 in. (20 cm)

MAMMALS

Common Raccoon
Procyon lotor To 40 in. (1 m)

Virginia Opossum
Didelphis virginiana To 40 in. (1 m)

Bottlenosed Dolphin
Tursiops truncatus To 12 ft. (3.6 m)

Humpback Whale
Megaptera novaeangliae To 50 ft. (15 m)
Long flippers have 'scalloped' edges.

Finback Whale
Balaenoptera physalus To 80 ft. (24 m)